Dates of a Decade

THE 1980s

Joseph Harris

with additional text by Jacqueline Laks Gorman

ARCTURUS

This edition first published by Arcturus Publishing
Distributed by Black Rabbit Books
123 South Broad Street
Mankato
Minnesota MN 56001

Series concept: Alex Woolf
Editor and picture researcher: Alex Woolf
U.S. editor: Jacqueline Laks Gorman
Designer: Phipps Design

Library of Congress Cataloging-in-Publication Data

Harris, Joseph, 1982-
  The 1980s / Joseph Harris.
    p. cm. -- (Dates of a decade)
  Includes index.
  ISBN 978-1-84837-284-9 (hardcover)
  1. History, Modern--1945-1989--Juvenile literature. I. Title.
  D848.H384 2010
  909.82'8--dc22
                    2009000008

Picture credits:
Corbis: cover *centre* (Neal Preston), cover *left* and 10, 13 (Roger Ressmeyer), 14
(Bettmann), 17 (David Rubinger), 18 (Bettmann), 19 (Jean Louis Atlan/Sygma), 22
(Peter Turnley), 23 (Peter Turnley), 24 (Reuters), 25 (Bettmann), 26, 27 (Bettmann),
28 (Igor Kostin/Sygma), 29 (Igor Kostin/Sygma), 30 (Reuters), 31 (CinemaPhoto), 32
(Reuters), 33 (Reuters), 36 (Peter Turnley), 37 (Bettmann), cover *right* and 38
(Reuters), 39 (David Turnley), 41 (Neal Preston), 42 (Doug Mills/Bettmann), 43
(Bettmann), 44 (Roy Corral), 45 (Gary Braasch).
Getty Images: 4, 5 (Popperfoto), 6 (AFP), 7 (AFP), 9, 11 (Time & Life Pictures), 12
(AFP), 15, 16 (AFP), 21 (AFP).
Shutterstock: 34 (Daniele DM), 35 (TAOLMOR).

Contents

GLOBAL EVENTS

UNITED STATES EVENTS

04
MARCH
1980

Mugabe Wins Zimbabwean Elections

The elections were the first to be held in Zimbabwe Rhodesia in which the black majority had an opportunity to take real power. The victory of Robert Mugabe and his ZANU (Zimbabwe African National Union) party marked the end of years of domination by the country's white minority. Not long before, Mugabe had been a guerrilla leader in the bush, hunted by government forces. Now he would become prime minister. Many people regarded him as a dangerous extremist, but the election result showed that the black majority overwhelmingly supported ZANU and rejected the past.

Illegal independence

Zimbabwe Rhodesia had been a British colony until 1965. It was known first as Southern Rhodesia and later simply as Rhodesia, after the British empire-builder Cecil Rhodes. The largely self-governing colony was ruled by the privileged white minority. In the 1960s, they began to fear that the British government would give the vote to the black majority and then grant the colony independence. To stop this from happening, in 1965 the Rhodesian government, led by Ian Smith, issued a Unilateral (one-sided) Declaration of Independence (UDI)

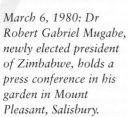

March 6, 1980: Dr Robert Gabriel Mugabe, newly elected president of Zimbabwe, holds a press conference in his garden in Mount Pleasant, Salisbury.

from Britain. The intention was clearly to keep Rhodesia under white control. Britain declared the UDI illegal, and most countries condemned Smith's racist regime. Sanctions (limits on trade) were imposed to hurt Rhodesia's economy, but Rhodesia was helped by similar, neighboring racist regimes, notably South Africa.

The regime weakens

Black Rhodesians responded by forming two guerrilla movements, Mugabe's ZANU and Joshua Nkomo's ZAPU. By the late 1970s, Smith's government was weakened by international pressure and long "bush wars" against the guerrillas, and it finally began to make concessions. Rhodesia was renamed Zimbabwe Rhodesia (after an ancient city built before whites settled the country) in 1979 and a black-majority government was elected, led by Bishop Abel Muzorewa. However, Smith had arranged matters so that real power remained in the hands of the whites. Finally, however, in early 1980, he was forced to allow elections in which power would pass to the winner and the guerrilla groups would take part. ZANU took 57 and ZAPU 20 of the 80 seats elected by the black population. The name "Rhodesia" was dropped and the country became Zimbabwe.

As prime minister, Mugabe promised to treat the white minority fairly. However, he failed to live up to his promises, and Zimbabwe was to suffer greatly from his increasingly despotic rule.

Jubilant supporters of Robert Mugabe celebrate his election victory and the transfer of real political power from a white elite to the black majority.

What the papers said

The great gamble in Zimbabwe Rhodesia is over. The result is presumably not what those who staked so much [Smith and his followers] can have hoped. They may nonetheless still hope that the consequences will not be as dire as might be expected. Mr. Mugabe is in fact an unknown quantity. How he will turn out is unpredictable, as it always seems to be with Africans who get power.... If Mr. Mugabe disappoints his friends and delights his opponents, he will not be the first African to do so. We must hope he will do both.

Daily Telegraph, March 5, 1980

- **FURTHER INFORMATION**
- 📖 Books:
  Africa: Postcolonial Conflict by David Downing (Heinemann, 2004)
- 🖰 Websites:
  news.bbc.co.uk/1/hi/world/africa/country_profiles/1064589.stm
  A good overview of the history, geography, and economy of the country

30 AUGUST 1980

Solidarity Is Legalized in Poland

On August 30, 1980, Poland's communist government gave in to pressure from striking workers who were demanding greater freedom. The deputy prime minister, Mieczyslaw Jagielski, met with the leader of the strike, Lech Walesa, and other workers' representatives in the northern city of Gdansk. They made the "Gdansk Agreement," which permitted workers to form their own trade union, independent of the state and free to take strike action. This was an extraordinary event since communist states normally refused to tolerate any kind of opposition and allowed only government-controled unions to operate.

The government's failure

In Poland, communism had been established in 1945, at the end of World War II, by the Soviet Union. Poland became part of the East European communist bloc. The Polish communists were in fact a small minority, and communism never became genuinely popular. However, it was economic failure that seriously undermined the government's authority in 1980. Living standards were already low, and in July, when the government increased the cost of basic commodities, discontent became serious.

At the Lenin shipyard in Gdansk, a popular crane operator, Anna Walentynowicz, was fired. For the disgruntled workforce, this was the final straw. An unemployed electrician named Lech Walesa emerged as the leader of the protesting workers, who occupied the shipyard. They held it for two months, resisting government attempts to divide them by making limited concessions. The news spread, and in August strikes sprang up across Poland.

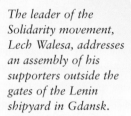

The leader of the Solidarity movement, Lech Walesa, addresses an assembly of his supporters outside the gates of the Lenin shipyard in Gdansk.

Solidarity

If the strikers had tried to fight the government, the army – or the Soviet Union – would have crushed them. Instead, they negotiated and sometimes cooperated with the authorities. For a time, the strategy worked. Following the Gdansk Agreement, the independent trade union Solidarity was formally established in September, with Walesa as its president. Millions of Poles joined it. However, the economic situation remained bleak and the Soviet Union pressed the Polish government to end the "Solidarity experiment," fearing that people in other communist countries might try to follow its example.

In December 1981, the Polish military, led by General Wojciech Jaruzelski, acted. They carried out mass arrests of Solidarity activists, proclaimed martial law, and drove Solidarity underground. Despite this, the movement had played an important role in showing the fragility of communist dictatorships. It reemerged in the late 1980s as East European communism collapsed. In 1990, Lech Walesa became the president of a free Poland.

Polish Prime Minister Wojciech Jaruzelski announces martial law during a televised address from Warsaw on December 13, 1981. The decree set up a new ruling body, the Military Council of National Salvation.

eye witness

The actual signing of the ... agreement was scheduled for the great assembly hall on Monday, August 31. With a minimum of ceremony both sides signed the papers.... On the Monday morning, the first trade union office was opened.... The rooms were on the first floor of a decrepit office block with creaking floorboards.... It was some months before the rest of the country was prepared to recognize the idea of free trade unions.... The capital of a new workers' Poland had moved to the Baltic coast.

Lech Walesa, *A Path of Hope* (Collins Harvill, 1987)

- **SEE ALSO**
  Pages 38–39: November 10, 1989
  The Berlin Wall Comes Down

- **FURTHER INFORMATION**
  📖 Books:
  Lech Walesa by Mary Craig
  (Watford, Exley, 1988)
  Websites:
  www.solidarity.gov.pl
  A multimedia site illustrating the history of Solidarity

22
SEPTEMBER
1980

Iran and Iraq Go to War

There had been skirmishes for some time between Iraqi and Iranian forces in their disputed border territories. Then, on September 22, Iraq suddenly launched air strikes on Iranian airfields and began a full-scale land invasion. Iran's air force struck back, and Iranian troops and militiamen were rushed to the front. Iraq's dictator, Saddam Hussein, hoped for a rapid victory, but the war turned into a long, bloody, and futile conflict.

The enemies

Iraq and Iran were both Muslim nations, but in important respects they were very different. Iraq was a secular state in which religion had relatively little influence on political policies. In contrast, Iran's supreme authority was a senior Muslim figure, the Ayatollah Khomeini, who had headed the country's "Islamic Revolution" in 1979. As a result, Iranian society was run on strict religious lines, and many aspects of the Western, and especially American, way of life were condemned and outlawed.

Since Khomeini wished to spread the Islamic Revolution to other lands, the United States and many other Western countries supported Iraq in the conflict. However, the Western nations had underestimated Saddam's ambition to control the Persian Gulf, which was the key to the region's vast oil wealth. The immediate cause of the conflict between Iraq and Iran was a shared waterway leading into the Gulf, the Shatt al-Arab, claimed by Iraq. Saddam also hoped to seize the oil-rich Iranian province of Khuzestan.

eye witness

We managed to catch glimpses of the Iranian Air Force in action here in Baghdad.… I was woken by a persistent sound ... like someone wearing hobnail boots clattering down a concrete staircase. It was, in fact, anti-aircraft fire echoing around the city and coming from batteries placed on buildings a hundred yards away. From my hotel balcony I saw two American-built Phantom jets flying at a tremendous speed straight at me.... At night the city is blacked out – we have to write our reports, this one included, by candlelight.

Michael Vestey in Tony Grant (editor), *From Our Own Correspondent* (Pan, 1995)

Stalemate

The Iraqi advance was soon halted and their forces were then driven back. By 1982, Saddam was ready to make peace and it was Iran that insisted on continuing the conflict. The war turned into a stalemate. Defensive lines, bristling with machine guns, prevented both sides from securing a permanent advantage. Both used any

Iraqi dictator Saddam Hussein addresses his forces before the invasion of Iran. The attack led to an eight-year war.

means available. Iraq employed chemical weapons, while the Iranians sent barely trained conscripts to advance in human waves against the enemy lines. Cities were subjected to aerial bombardment, causing many civilian casualties. Nothing could break the deadlock, and in 1988, the UN finally brokered a ceasefire.

In 1990, when Saddam invaded Kuwait and became the West's deadly enemy, he made peace with Iran. After the loss of a million or more lives, the frontiers remained the same as they had been in 1980.

- **SEE ALSO**
  Pages 42–43: November 25, 1986
  The Iran-Contra Affair Is Revealed

- **FURTHER INFORMATION**
  📖 Books:
  Saddam Hussein and Iraq by David Downing (Heinemann, 2004)
  🌐 Websites:
  encarta.msn.com/encnet/refpages/
  RefArticle.aspx?refid=761580640
  An accessible outline of the war

Reagan Is Elected U.S. President

On November 4, 1980, the Republican Party's candidate, Ronald Reagan, swept to victory in the U.S. presidential election. He trounced the sitting president, Democrat Jimmy Carter, so thoroughly that Carter conceded defeat even before polling had finished in some places. Carter had come to be seen as a weak leader, especially since he had failed to rescue U.S. hostages held in Iran. Reagan was 69, a former Hollywood actor and governor of California. Though relaxed and soft-spoken, he seemed a tough character who offered the United States strong leadership.

The Cold War

Reagan was sworn in as president on January 20, 1981. He had a notable early success, reaching a deal with Iran that secured the release of the hostages. He also made important changes in U.S. foreign policy. Since 1945, two superpowers, the United States and the communist Soviet Union, had competed for global supremacy. Each possessed an arsenal of fearsomely destructive weapons. Despite a long "Cold War" of hostility and suspicion, the United States and the Soviet Union had not come to blows, and in the 1970s there had even been some easing of tensions between them.

Ronald Reagan and his wife Nancy wave to supporters on January 20, 1981, celebrating the new president's inauguration.

Reagan, however, was militantly anti-communist. He labeled the Soviet Union the "evil empire" and supported anti-communist groups all round the world. He even adopted a controversial plan – nicknamed "Star Wars" – to construct a defensive system in space. Though critics of Reagan's policies felt that they risked a world war, they came at a time when the Soviet Union was in economic decline and in no position to respond aggressively. In fact, during his second term as president, Reagan negotiated significant arms reductions with the Soviet Union. By the time he left office in 1989, the Cold War was coming to an end.

"Reaganomics"

Reagan also changed the direction of government policy at home. His ideas, often described as "Reaganomics," reflected the views of many conservatives. Reagan believed that the government interfered too much in people's lives. He wanted less regulation of business activity and favored tax cuts to encourage people to buy more and stimulate economic growth. Supporters of these policies held that, in the long run, they would benefit everybody, whereas critics argued that while they made the rich richer, the poor were left behind. Reagan's policies were similar to those of Margaret Thatcher in Britain and helped set the tone for the "consumerist" 1980s.

President Ronald Reagan (right) and Soviet leader Mikhail Gorbachev sign an arms reduction agreement in the East Room of the White House.

⊙ eye witness

It is painful even now to recall those last two days of the campaign, and the dismal results that I had to face on election night. After ... it became clear that the hostages [in Iran] would not be freed, Rosalynn [Carter's wife] and I knew my support had sharply fallen ... we did not anticipate the magnitude of our defeat. To lose all but six states and to have our party rejected ... were additional embarrassments for me.... At least it was a relief that the political campaign was over.

Jimmy Carter, *Keeping Faith* **(Collins, 1982)**

• **SEE ALSO**
Pages 22–23: March 11, 1985
Gorbachev Becomes Soviet Leader
Pages 42–43: November 25, 1986
The Iran-Contra Affair Is Revealed

• **FURTHER INFORMATION**
📖 Books:
Presidents by James Barber
(Dorling Kindersley, 2000)
Websites:
www.whitehouse.gov/history/presidents/rr40.html
A site with a biography and links to the Ronald Reagan archives

The IBM PC Is Released

On August 12, 1981, the world's leading computer manufacturer, IBM, announced that it had developed a new product, the personal computer, or PC. It was said to be an affordable computer system that would appeal to home users and small businesses. Rival companies, such as Commodore, Atari, and Apple, had already released machines aimed at these markets, but the IBM machine was the direct ancestor of the PCs used today. In fact the term PC now describes only computers that are "IBM compatible" – able to run the same programs as IBMs.

The 1981 IBM PC appears primitive compared to today's computers, but was cutting-edge technology at the time.

There have been many such machines, thanks to IBM's decision not to use all their own components. Instead, hurrying to develop their PC, they built it with parts bought from other manufacturers such as Intel, and software provided by Microsoft. Other corporations were free to buy such products and use them in their own PCs. Consequently, the PC market became highly competitive, forcing the pace of change.

The computer age

By the early 1980s, computers were able to handle huge amounts of information at a speed that humans could not match. Their impact on every aspect of human activity was bound to be immense. Very powerful computers had been developed before the 1980s, but the machines were very large and expensive, and operating them required special skills. Only governments and big corporations used them. The development of the PC in the 1980s was to make computers part of everyday life.

The PC revolution

Despite its lower price, the first IBM PC was still too expensive for most home users, but it sold in unexpectedly large numbers to businesses. This marked the beginning of a workplace revolution that accelerated as computers became increasingly user-friendly. The PC's word-processing programs made it possible to correct and reorganize text and information, and they swiftly replaced typewriters. Similarly, computer databases replaced paper-based systems of data storage.

PCs continued to become cheaper and more powerful, and by the later 1980s, PCs were invading the home, offering not only word processing but also increasingly complex and ingenious games. The microprocessors that lay at the heart of the IBM PC also allowed the development of other technologies. Many of these, such as cell phones and portable CD players, became familiar features of everyday life.

PCs very quickly became standard office equipment. This photo, from 1986, shows workers at a U.S. Internal Revenue Service office entering data from tax forms into computers.

What the papers said

International Business Machines of the U.S., the leader in the world market for large computers, yesterday made its long-awaited entry into the booming market for personal computers. The company unveiled a small machine, called the IBM Personal Computer, which will sell for only $1,565 in its most basic version and up to about $6,000 with all the trimmings. The computer industry has been speculating for months about the IBM machine, which will provide formidable competition for many products already on the market.

Ian Hargreaves, *Financial Times*, August 13, 1981

• **SEE ALSO**
Pages 24–25: July 13, 1985
The Live Aid Concerts
Pages 30-31: October 19, 1987
World Stock Exchanges Crash

• **FURTHER INFORMATION**

📖 Books:
The History of the Computer by Elizabeth Raum (Heinemann, 2008)

🖱 Websites:
inventors.about.com/library/blcoindex.htm
Covers the major developments in computer technology

Argentina Invades the Falklands

Early in the morning of April 2, 1982, the Argentines landed at three places on the main island, East Falkland. The 940 Argentines, equipped with troop carriers and transport vehicles, faced 81 British defenders, most of them Royal Marines. The first attack occurred at 5:30 A.M. By 9:30, the British, surrounded in Government House, had surrendered. The only casualties were one dead and two wounded Argentines.

Disputed sovereignty

The Falklands island group lies in the South Atlantic, 280 miles (450 kilometres) off the coast of Argentina. Their British-descended inhabitants wanted the Falklands to remain a British colony. The Argentines argued that, geographically, the islands were part of their country, stolen by the British. After years of talks, Argentina's ruling junta (military council) acted. In power since 1976, the junta had murdered thousands of opponents and was deeply unpopular. It invaded the Falklands in the hope of winning support for the régime, and the Argentine people did in fact greet the news with wild patriotic enthusiasm. The junta calculated that the British government would protest but would not fight for a group of far-away, insignificant islands.

A rally is held in the Plaza de Mayo in the Argentine capital, Buenos Aires, to boost morale following the British recapture of South Georgia on April 19.

The war

The junta was wrong. The British government, led by Margaret Thatcher, sent a fleet carrying 30,000 troops. It sailed the 8,078 miles (13,000 kilometres) to the Falklands and recaptured the islands in June 1982, along with the even more remote island of South Georgia, which the Argentines had also occupied.

The heaviest casualties occurred during engagements at sea. The Argentines made effective use of Exocet missiles, sinking the British destroyer HMS *Sheffield*. However, the Argentine navy was not strong enough to face the British fleet in battle. Britain defined an "exclusion zone" – any Argentine vessel appearing in this area would be deemed a legitimate target. In the war's most controversial incident, a British submarine sank the Argentine cruiser *General Belgrano*, with 323 hands lost, although the vessel was outside the exclusion zone and heading away from it. However, the *General Belgrano* was under orders to attack the British navy and, in 1994, the Argentine government conceded that the sinking was a legal act of war. On land, British troops overcame the Argentine forces after some sharp encounters, notably at Goose Green.

The aftermath

Compared with most wars, the death toll (fewer than 1,000) was small. The political consequences were important, however. Victory boosted the fortunes of Margaret Thatcher's previously unpopular government and helped her to win the 1983 election. In contrast, the humiliation of defeat destroyed the junta. Its head, General Leopoldo Galtieri, resigned, and the junta itself collapsed soon afterward. By 1983, Argentina had returned to democracy.

A line of British soldiers advances during the campaign to win back the Falklands. In all, 258 British troops lost their lives in the conflict.

eye witness

It all went just as though we were on an exercise.... My group of four Amtracs [armored troop carriers] approached the beach in a diamond formation. If I got ashore safely, the others would form a column and follow me in.... All went well. The beach was incredibly white, to my surprise, with a steep slope 10 meters (33 feet) from the waterline, a few rocks; there was no cover for my huge Amtrac, and I thought I was a sitting duck as I came up that slope – but the place was deserted.

Lieutenant-Commander Hugo Santillón, in Martin Middlebrook, *The Argentine Fight for the Falklands* (Pen & Sword Books, 2003)

• **FURTHER INFORMATION**
📖 Books:
   Argentina by Les and Daisy Fearns (Evans, 2005)
🖰 Websites:
   www.falklandswar.org.uk/
   A site with photos and personal accounts of the conflict

Massacres in Lebanon

Between September 16 and 18, militias linked with a Lebanese political party, the Phalange, carried out massacres that horrified the world. The victims were Palestinian refugees who lived in two camps, Sabra and Shatila, on the edge of the Lebanese capital, Beirut. The condition of the corpses showed that the killings had been carried out in a particularly savage fashion. Entire families, including children, had been wiped out. The number of deaths was never reliably established, and estimates ranged between 700 and 3,500.

Turmoil in Lebanon

At this time, Lebanon was in a chaotic state. Lebanese political life was based on Christians and Muslims sharing power, but this arrangement was showing signs of breaking down. The situation was complicated by the existence of camps like Sabra and Shatila, housing Palestinian refugees from neighboring Israel. The camps also served as bases for the PLO (Palestine Liberation Organization), which conducted cross-border terrorist and guerrilla operations against Israel. The PLO also played a part in the power struggles within Lebanon, in conflict with Christian militias such as the Phalangists.

A Palestinian woman weeps as the body of one of her relatives is carried away on a stretcher following the Phalangist assault on the Sabra refugee camp.

Invasion and massacres

In June 1982, Israeli forces invaded Lebanon to drive out the PLO. The Christian militias were their allies. The Israelis besieged the PLO's strongholds in West Beirut until the PLO agreed to leave the country. By September, the PLO's forces had been shipped out under international supervision. However, the Israelis suspected that there were still PLO elements in Sabra and Shatila, and the Phalangist militia was sent in to flush them out. Instead, the militiamen began a wholesale massacre, probably acting in revenge for the assassination three weeks before of a newly installed Phalangist president of Lebanon, Bashir Gemayel.

The fallout

The massacre raised serious questions about the role of the Israeli army. Were the militiamen sent in just to weed out terrorists, or did the Israelis know what was going to happen? Why didn't the army step in once the killing had started? Some 300,000 Israelis demonstrated in the streets, demanding answers. An official investigation blamed the defense minister, Ariel Sharon, for failing to foresee how the Phalangists were likely to behave. Sharon resigned, although he later made a remarkable comeback as prime minister in 2001. The Phalangist leaders were never brought to justice. Lebanon remained a flashpoint of Middle Eastern violence.

Israelis demonstrate outside the home of their prime minister, Menachem Begin, after the massacre in Beirut.

What the papers said

There are many versions of the massacre.... Some of the victims were lying among ... half-packed suitcases as if they had been trying to escape when the killers burst in. Others had obviously been taken by surprise, because there were half-eaten meals near the bodies.... Reporters said it was impossible to get an accurate estimate of the numbers of Palestinians killed because the bodies were strewn across several acres of wreckage.... Bulldozers had been used to pile wreckage on many of the bodies in an attempt to conceal them, but arms and legs were sticking out of the rubble.

Colin Smith and Eric Silver, Observer, September 19, 1982

- **SEE ALSO**
  Pages 36–37: June 4, 1989
  Massacre in Tiananmen Square

- **FURTHER INFORMATION**
  📖 Books:
  The Middle East: Israel and Palestine by John King (Heinemann, 2005)
  🔗 Websites:
  www.globaleye.org.uk/secondary_spring06/ eyeon/palestinians.html
  The plight of Palestinian refugees in Lebanon, with lots of useful links

The HIV Virus Is Identified

On April 23, 1984, U.S. Health Secretary Margaret Heckler announced that scientists had identified the cause of the fearful disease Aids (Acquired Immune Deficiency Syndrome). It was a virus, given the name HIV (Human Immunodeficiency Virus). HIV infected white blood cells in the bloodstream and prevented them from fighting infections. It also implanted the cells with its own genetic material, enabling the virus to multiply. The final stage of the infection, AIDS, did not kill sufferers directly. They died because of the damage done to their bodies' natural defenses (the immune system), which meant that even slight infections could prove fatal.

The identification of HIV was not an exclusively American feat – a French team had achieved similar results in 1983. Credit for the discovery is now shared between scientists of the two nations. It was hailed as a major breakthrough and encouraged hopes that a cure might rapidly be found.

The first cases

AIDS first came to public attention in 1981 as a nameless disorder. Previously healthy homosexual men in three American cities, Los Angeles, San Francisco, and New York, showed symptoms such as extreme weight loss, leading eventually to death, often from a lung infection or rare skin cancer. Over 150 cases were identified during 1981. At first, people believed the disease affected only homosexuals. Subsequently, the disease was discovered in some heterosexuals.

The disease was passed on through contact with infected blood and could be contracted through sexual intercourse or, in the case of drug users, by sharing the needles they used to

At a joint press conference, Dr. Robert Gallo, a researcher at the National Cancer Institute, and Margaret Heckler, the U.S. Health secretary, announce that the HIV virus has been identified. Gallo led the American team that made the discovery.

The enormous AIDS Memorial Quilt was created to commemorate AIDS victims. Begun in 1987 in San Francisco, it is shown here during a public display in Washington, D.C.

inject themselves. An infected mother could pass it to her child during pregnancy or breastfeeding. Before the dangers became apparent, some individuals contracted the disease from transfusions of infected blood.

Global epidemic

By 1985, when the World Health Organization defined AIDS as an epidemic, the disease was causing widespread anxiety. Governments ran education programs to combat misinformation and promote the use of condoms for "safe sex." The first treatments – not cures – appeared, but the high cost of the drugs involved were beyond the means of many poorer sufferers. Although millions were suffering globally, Africa was the hardest hit, probably because AIDS had been present there for the longest time. From the 1990s, the AIDS issue was being raised everywhere from the United Nations to pop concerts. Hopes of an early cure faded, and the world faced a long and painful battle against the disease.

What the papers said

The multi-million dollar hunt for the cause of AIDS may soon be over but the epidemic is likely to continue spreading at an ever-increasing rate for two years or more. Barring a breakthrough in treatment, the recent discoveries by U.S. and French scientists will have come too late to save the 2,000 surviving AIDS victims and the 3,000 or more people in Europe and the US who on current trends will develop the disease this year.... The number of U.S. cases topped 4,000 this month.

Andrew Veitch, *Guardian*, April 25, 1984

• **FURTHER INFORMATION**

📖 Books:
HIV and AIDS by Andrew Campbell (Watts, 2004)

🖰 Websites:
library.thinkquest.org/J003087F/
An all-you-need-to-know site for young people

31 OCTOBER 1984

India's Prime Minister Is Assassinated

The Indian prime minister, Indira Gandhi, was murdered on October 31, 1984 by her own bodyguards. They shot her as she left her New Delhi home to meet a TV crew. The assassins were Sikhs, members of a minority religion in India, where the majority are Hindus. The killing sparked widespread violence against Sikhs, and it was in a climate of disorder that Gandhi's son Rajiv was sworn in as her successor. She was cremated three days later.

Operation Blue Star

Since achieving independence from Britain in 1947, India had enjoyed stability as the world's largest democracy. But it was a land of many peoples and religions, which sometimes created serious problems. Indira Gandhi's assassination was an act of revenge, prompted by a military operation she had authorized four months earlier. The operation was directed against Sikh militants who aimed to win independence for their home region, the Punjab, and used terrorism to achieve their goal.

In June 1984, Indian troops surrounded the terrorist leader Jarnail Singh Bhindranwale and his followers, who had taken refuge in the Golden Temple in Amritsar. The temple was the Sikhs' holiest shrine, but after a three-day siege the Indian forces launched a direct attack. The assault, Operation Blue Star, met with ferocious resistance. Over 700 of the militants were killed in the fighting, and the temple was damaged. Many Sikhs were outraged. Among them were the previously loyal guards who killed Indira Gandhi.

What the papers said

Mrs. Gandhi was killed in the gardens of her own home as she walked towards ... her staff offices.... As she came towards her assassins, two of them greeted her with a ... bow with hands pressed together; she returned the traditional greeting. Sub-Inspector Beant Singh of the Delhi Armed Police, fired at her with his revolver.... Constable Satwant Singh emptied 30 rounds of his Sten gun at her as she lay on the ground. Both he and Inspector Beant were themselves shot by other guards.

Michael Hamlyn, *The Times*, November 1, 1984

*India's new premier,
Rajiv Gandhi (at the front of the
group with his wife and daughter), stands
before the cremation pyre of his mother, Indira
Gandhi, in New Delhi.*

A new era

When Rajiv Gandhi took office, he appealed for an end to the violence
against Sikhs. He went on to grant the Sikhs a degree of autonomy (self-
rule, but not independence) and offered to repair the Golden Temple. This
calmed the situation, although neither Sikh nor Hindu extremists were
satisfied. As prime minister, Rajiv Gandhi broke with the policies of Indira
Gandhi and her father, Jawaharlal Nehru, who between them had ruled
India for almost the entire period since 1947. Under their
leadership, many aspects of the Indian economy had been
state controled, and India had been neutral in
international affairs and friendly with the Soviet
Union. Rajiv promoted a more competitive, less
regulated economy and moved closer to the United
States. The death of Indira Gandhi marked the end of
an era. However, the Nehru "dynasty" continued to
dominate Indian politics in the person of Rajiv
Gandhi, until he too was assassinated in 1991.

• **FURTHER INFORMATION**
📖 Books:
Indira Gandhi by Anita Ganeri (Heinemann, 2003)
🖰 Websites:
www.sikh-history.com/sikhhist/events/
attack841.html
Operation Blue Star

Gorbachev Becomes Soviet Leader

On March 11, 1985, Mikhail Gorbachev became general secretary of the Central Committee of the Soviet Communist Party, a post that made him the leader of the Soviet Union. At 54, Gorbachev was comparatively young. The Soviet leaders before him, Yuri Andropov and Konstantin Chernenko, had been elderly men who had ruled for only a short time before dying. Gorbachev was chosen because of a general recognition that dynamic leadership was needed to reenergize a stagnant Soviet Union.

Soviet problems

The Soviet Union was dominated by the Communist Party, which suppressed all opposition and made any political changes difficult to achieve. Some past crimes and mistakes, especially under the dictatorship of Joseph Stalin (1928–1953), had been admitted. But much was still covered up, and the Soviet Union remained a secretive society. Moreover, by the 1970s, the country was suffering from severe economic problems.

The Soviet Union's centralized, state-run economy was highly inefficient and struggled to cope with the pressures of its military rivalry with the United States. The Soviet Union led an alliance of communist states in competition with the United States and its allies. In this "Cold War," both sides spent vast sums on nuclear and other armaments, as well as propping up weaker allies and seeking to influence uncommitted nations. By the mid-1980s, around 15–17 percent of the Soviet Union's gross national product (total value of all its goods and services) was spent on defense.

Soviet Premier Mikhail Gorbachev greets an enthusiastic crowd in Prague in the former Czechoslovakia.

Gorbachev's reforms

To tackle the problems, Gorbachev proclaimed new policies of perestroika (restructuring the Soviet economy) and glasnost (openness). The economy was decentralized, giving local authorities and businesspeople more responsibility. Facts about the country's past and present were revealed. People were encouraged to express themselves freely and were promised greater choice in electing their leaders. Gorbachev sought agreement with the United States on ending the nuclear arms race, and he reduced the size of the Soviet armed forces. Soviet aid to friends and allies was also cut, and Gorbachev made it clear that Soviet troops would no longer be used to rescue unpopular communist regimes.

Communist collapse

Gorbachev wished to reform, not destroy, the communist system. But economic decentralization at home was mismanaged and weakened the country further. In 1989, the communist regimes of Eastern Europe collapsed, no longer supported by the Soviet Union. The Soviet Union itself survived until 1991, when it – and Gorbachev's own career – came to an end.

Gorbachev's poorly planned reforms led to an economic crisis. Lines outside shops were a common sight as essential goods became increasingly scarce.

⊙ eye witness

On March 10, 1985, I had barely returned home after work when the telephone rang and … informed me of Chernenko's death. After the call I … convened [called] a Politburo meeting for 11 P.M. that night.… It was about four o'clock in the morning when I returned home. Raisa Maksimova [his wife] was waiting up for me … my last words that night stand out in my mind: "You see … if I really want to change something I would have to accept the nomination [as general secretary].… We can't go on living like this."

Mikhail Gorbachev, *Memoirs* (Doubleday, 1996)

• **SEE ALSO**
Pages 32-33: February 15, 1989
Soviet Troops Leave Afghanistan
Pages 38-39: November 10, 1989
The Berlin Wall Comes Down

• **FURTHER INFORMATION**
📖 Books:
Mikhail Gorbachev by Andrew Langley
(Heinemann, 2003)
⌁ Websites:
www.achievement.org/autodoc/page/gor0int-1
An interview with Gorbachev

The Live Aid Concerts

Two groundbreaking televised concerts were held on July 13, 1985 to raise money for famine victims in Africa. The event was called "Live Aid" and was the brainchild of Bob Geldof, lead singer of the band the Boomtown Rats. Live Aid was the biggest pop event of all time. The performances at London's Wembley Stadium and Philadelphia's John F. Kennedy Stadium were broadcast across the world via satellite and reached a global audience of over 1.5 billion people in 160 countries. In a single day, the campaign received $70 million in donations for its charitable work. Among the performers were Dire Straits, Queen, Madonna, David Bowie, and Mick Jagger. Live Aid demonstrated the power of music to promote awareness of problems, especially now that recent advances in technology had made it possible to reach such gigantic audiences.

Music and idealism

The lyrics of popular songs have often carried political messages, demanding change or denouncing injustice. However, such messages were less common in the music of the early 1980s, an era when the pursuit of personal wealth and happiness were emphasized. The mood was reflected in the light-hearted music of the New Romantics, including popular performers like Duran Duran and Wham! A group such as Frankie Goes to Hollywood was exceptional in

Live Aid performers take the stage together for the concert finale. Among those who can be seen are Paul McCartney, Freddie Mercury, David Bowie, Howard Jones, Adam Ant, and Bob Geldof.

24

raising issues such as the threat of nuclear war. American hip-hop acts also took a new direction by drawing attention to the plight of inner-city black people. But the big breakthrough was the release of the 1984 Band Aid single "Do They Know It's Christmas?," produced by Bob Geldof to raise money for starving Ethiopians. Its success was the inspiration for the Live Aid event the following year.

New media

In the 1980s, changes in technology reshaped the music industry. Acts in one country could now be seen across the globe. A new cable channel, Music Television (MTV), transmitted music videos continuously, and it became essential for singles to be supported by an eye-catching video. Also in the 1980s, music managers began to artificially create certain acts, selecting the members and molding their look, music, and style to appeal to a particular market. While the global exposure provided by videos allowed new acts to reach unprecedented audiences, the arrival of CDs (compact discs) gave older performers the opportunity to resell their albums, and the music industry boomed.

Some of the 90,000 rock fans watching the U.S. portion of the Live Aid Concert at John F. Kennedy Stadium in Philadelphia.

eye witness

There was a tremendous feeling of oneness on that stage. There had been no rivalry, no bitching, no displays of temperament all day. Now everyone was singing. They had their arms around each other.... Elton [John] was crying, everyone was crying. Not the easy tears of showbiz but genuine emotion.... The performance was still a shambles but perhaps the audience were prepared for that.... Well, the world sang it. "Feed the World" exploded out of that stadium and literally shot around the planet.... It was a moment that let millions live. "Remember this day," I wrote later.

Bob Geldof, *Is That It?* (Sidgwick and Jackson, 1986)

- **SEE ALSO**
  Pages 12–13: August 12, 1981
  The IBM PC Is Released
  Pages 40–41: August 1, 1981
  MTV Debuts

- **FURTHER INFORMATION**
  📖 Books:
  1980s Pop by Bob Brunning (Heinemann, 1998)
  🖱 Websites:
  www.bbc.co.uk/music/thelive8event/liveaid/
  history.shtml
  Memories of the Live Aid concert

Space Shuttle Challenger Explodes

At 11:38 A.M. on January 28, 1986, the latest U.S. space mission was launched. It ended in tragedy 73 seconds later. The space shuttle Challenger broke up at a height of 9.3 miles (15 kilometres) and a speed of about 2,175 miles (3,500 kilometres) per hour. The shuttle's crew of seven were killed. Among them was a schoolteacher, Christa McAuliffe, chosen as the first civilian to be sent into space. The Challenger crew were the first Americans to die in space. The disaster led to questions about NASA's safety procedures and the future of the space shuttle program.

A thick cloud of engine exhaust, solid rocket booster plume, and expanding gas fill the sky above the Kennedy Space Center in Florida after the explosion of the space shuttle Challenger, which claimed the lives of seven crew members.

Why it happened

The cause of the disaster turned out to be a faulty seal (O-ring) on one of the shuttle's booster rockets. A tongue of flame escaped, as video footage of the launch revealed. The breach in the booster disrupted the external fuel tank and caused the craft to break up. NASA later admitted that the booster rockets had no sensors to warn of problems. Moreover, the launch was allowed to proceed even though some engineers expressed their concern about the low temperature on launch day – the O-ring component that failed could not be relied upon if it was too cold. The mission had already been rescheduled several times as a result of delays and bad weather. The huge cost of the space program meant that repeated delays and failures would strengthen the case of critics who saw it as a waste of resources. So on January 28, NASA decided to ignore the doubters and proceed – with catastrophic results.

The shuttle suspended

The shuttle was introduced in 1981 as a reuseable space vehicle, differing from earlier spacecraft in its ability to leave earth and return intact. Until 1986, it had enjoyed an excellent record. Following the accident, shuttle flights were suspended while an investigation took place. Part of the blame was attributed to NASA's faulty internal communications and decision-making processes. The disaster was a blow to confidence in the space program, and it was almost three years before another shuttle was launched.

However, there were also positive developments in the exploration of space during the 1980s, notably the journeys made by the unmanned probes Voyager I and Voyager II. Launched back in 1977, the Voyager probes sent back the first high-resolution images of Saturn (1980–1981), Uranus (1986), and Neptune (1989), planets in the outer regions of the solar system.

The seven-person crew of the Challenger included the first civilian selected to go into space, Christa McAuliffe (back row, second from the left).

What the papers said

The Challenger lifted off flawlessly this morning ... for what was to have been the 25th mission.... The ship rose for about a minute on a column of smoke and fire from its five engines. Suddenly, without warning, it erupted in a ball of flame.... The eerie beauty of the orange fireball and billowing white trails ... confused many onlookers.... There were few sobs, moans or shouts among the thousands of tourists, reporters, and space agency officials ... just a stunned silence as they began to realize that the Challenger had vanished.

William J. Broad, *New York Times*, January 28, 1986

• **FURTHER INFORMATION**
📖 Books:
Challenger 1986, the Space Shuttle Explodes by Liz Gogerly (Raintree, 2006)
⌨ Websites:
www.nasa.gov/mission_pages/shuttle/shuttlemissions/archives/sts-51L.html
NASA's own account of the disaster

26 APRIL 1986

Accident at Chernobyl

The world's worst nuclear accident occurred at the Chernobyl nuclear power plant in Ukraine, in the southern Soviet Union, on April 26, 1986. A reactor at the plant exploded, and deadly radioactive material escaped. At first the Soviet authorities tried to keep the disaster secret. Four days passed before they admitted that there had been an "incident," and even then they downplayed its seriousness. However, the rest of the world quickly became aware of it. Unusually high radiation levels were observed in Scandinavia, and U.S. satellite photos revealed that the top of the reactor had been blown off. Soviet firefighters struggled to contain the blaze. Lacking proper protective equipment, many of them died from the effects of the radiation. Efforts to contain the disaster and prevent it from spreading continued into mid-May.

Global fears

On May 14, the Soviet leader, Mikhail Gorbachev, appeared on television. He admitted that 299 people had been killed in the explosion and that many more were suffering from radiation exposure. Winds carried the radioactive matter across the Soviet border into northern Europe. Scandinavia and Finland were particularly badly affected, and the Sami people of the far north found their entire way of life threatened when the

Disaster at Chernobyl: at the nuclear power plant in Ukraine, the overheating core of reactor number 4 caused the entire roof to be blown off the building.

These apples, hanging from a tree near Chernobyl, were visibly contaminated as a result of the disaster at the city's nuclear plant. The city itself had to be abandoned and is still a ghost town.

reindeer on which they depended became contaminated. European governments placed restrictions on the movement and sale of livestock and other products. Some of these restrictions were still in force 20 years later.

Dangerous power

Chernobyl was not the first nuclear accident. Many smaller incidents had occurred in the past. In 1979, there was a major alarm at Three Mile Island in Pennsylvania, which caused the United States to suspend its program of building new power stations. Chernobyl was truly disastrous, however. The entire area around the power station, including the city of Chernobyl, had to be evacuated and sealed off.

The long-term effects of the accident were much disputed. One report gave a low figure of 4,000 deaths worldwide resulting from the accident. Others suggested that radiation, responsible for cancers and birth defects, had had a huge impact across Europe. The issue remained relevant in the 2000s. When some experts argued for an expansion of nuclear energy as an alternative to fossil fuels, others pointed out the dangers of nuclear accidents, using Chernobyl as an example.

⊙ eye witness

We were newlyweds.... We lived in the fire station where he worked.... One night I heard a noise. I looked out the window. He saw me.... "Go back to sleep. There's a fire at the reactor. I'll be back soon." I didn't see the explosion itself. Just the flames. Everything was radiant. The whole sky. A tall flame. And smoke. The heat was awful.... At seven in the morning I was told he was in the hospital. He was all swollen and puffed up.... I tell the nurse: "He's dying." And she says: "What did you expect? He got 1,600 roentgen. Four hundred is a lethal dose."

Lyudmilla Ignatenko, in Svetlana Alexievich, *Voices from Chernobyl* (Dalkey Archive, 2005)

- **SEE ALSO**
Pages 22–23: March 11, 1985
Gorbachev Becomes Soviet Leader

- **FURTHER INFORMATION**
📖 Books:
When Disaster Struck: Chernobyl by Vic Parker (Heinemann, 2006)

🖳 Websites:
library.thinkquest.org/3426/
A comprehensive site about the disaster

World Stock Exchanges Crash

October 19, 1987 is remembered as "Black Monday," a day that witnessed a huge drop in the value of shares in financial markets across the world. The fall began on Friday October 16, with heavy selling on Wall Street in New York City, the principal U.S. stock exchange and the world's most influential center of finance. When large numbers of people want to get rid of their shares, prices fall and the shares are worth less. If the selling continues, share values fall low enough to hurt or even ruin individuals and companies. This was what happened after stock exchanges reopened on Monday morning. The selling continued and share prices fell in Tokyo, London, Hong Kong, and Wall Street.

Shock and fear

The crash was so severe that people feared there would be a world depression. This had happened in 1929, when the Wall Street crash triggered a shrinking of the world economy and mass unemployment. Fortunately, in 1987, the follow-up to Black Monday proved to be less disastrous. Afterward, there was no agreement as to the cause of the crash. Over-rapid expansion and an over-optimism that pushed prices too high were common explanations. Some blamed recently installed computer systems that were pre-programmed to buy and sell shares.

Frantic traders on the floor of the Sydney Stock Exchange try to sell off their shares before the close of trading. More than 60 billion Australian dollars were wiped off the market's value in one day, a record in the history of the exchange.

What the papers said

The rumors mounted by the hour as Wall Street lunged and lurched through its wildest week. Many of the country's biggest ... firms ... were said to be in trouble, even sinking.... Even before Black Monday struck, there were signs that Wall Street's five-year stay in Fat City was ending. Profits were shrinking.... Retrenchment [economizing] of some kind was already in the cards. Last week's crash guaranteed that it will be harsher than was previously expected. There is plenty of shrinking to do.... What had happened was, in a word, overexpansion.

John Greenwald, *Time*, November 2, 1987

They argued that this "program trading" could lead to unwise mass selling, with disastrous results. However, there was no evidence that human traders would have behaved differently, since chain-reaction selling had often occurred in earlier crises.

Enterprise culture

During the 1980s, acquiring personal wealth became a central value for many people in Western society. President Ronald Reagan in the United States and Britain's Margaret Thatcher were particularly active in encouraging an "enterprise culture." They stressed the importance of risk-taking and profit-making as engines of economic growth. Critics of these values argued that they promoted selfishness and greed at the expense of social responsibility. Many people certainly did very well in this period, including the high-earning young people often described as yuppies (Young, Upwardly Mobile Professionals). Loathed by some and admired by others, the typical yuppie would wear a pinstripe suit, have slicked-back hair, and drive an expensive sports car. Black Monday was a major blow to the self-assurance of these products of the enterprise culture.

Charlie Sheen in the 1987 film Wall Street. *The movie is regarded as a classic portrayal of 1980s greed. Sheen plays an ambitious yuppie.*

- **SEE ALSO**
  Pages 10–11: December 4, 1980
  Reagan Is Elected U.S. President
  Pages 12–13: August 12, 1981
  The IBM PC Is Released

- **FURTHER INFORMATION**
  Books:
  What Happens in the Stock Exchange by Soraya Moeng (Watts, 2000)
  Websites:
  www.ft.com/indepth/blackmonday
  A site with links to videos explaining the crash

Soviet Troops Leave Afghanistan

The last remaining Soviet units in Afghanistan began to leave on February 15, 1989. Their withdrawal ended a nine-year involvement in Afghanistan's internal struggles. It began in 1979, when Afghanistan was ruled by the communist PDPA (People's Democratic Party of Afghanistan). The government was facing a widespread rebellion and needed help from its Soviet ally. But when Soviet troops arrived in force, they overthrew the Afghan government in favor of a different faction of the PDPA.

The rapid build-up of Soviet military strength in Afghanistan was internationally condemned as an invasion, but the Soviet Union appeared determined to impose communism on an unwilling people. Their actions were not unprecedented. Both Cold War rivals, the United States and the Soviet Union, had often intervened, openly or secretly, in other countries to help allied governments or topple unfriendly regimes.

Soldiers of the Soviet Union's Red Army wave to onlookers as their convoy of armored vehicles makes its way out of Afghanistan.

⊙ eye witness

I was held at the airport for three days, in a small locked room.... I saw the last Soviet plane leave, with no ceremony and the last few gaudily made-up wives grumbling their way out across the tarmac.... I suppose it was a world exclusive as I was the only journalist there ... but I had no chance of filing a story: the military might have satellite phones in the 1980s, but journalists didn't.... I had no idea if anyone knew that the last Soviet plane had left Kabul. I was in the back of the beyond.

Jeremy Bowen, *War Stories* (Simon & Schuster, 2006)

The resistance

The new, Soviet-backed government failed to win over the people. Afghanistan was an economically backward country. Its people were Muslim and fiercely independent. Most were opposed to communism and hated foreign troops. The government often acted in a clumsy and brutal fashion. Measures such as land reform and the education of women found no support outside the towns.

The Soviet and Afghan armies easily won battles against local warlords, but rebel guerrillas were a different matter. These mujahideen, or "warriors," fought in small groups, taking advantage of Afghanistan's mountainous terrain to hit their enemies and then disappear. The United States supplied the mujahideen with anti-aircraft missiles and other weapons. Muslim fighters from other lands joined them in the fight. Like the United States in Vietnam, the Soviet Union became bogged down in a punishing and exhausting war it could not win. Eventually, the Soviet leader Mikhail Gorbachev decided to end the war. Soviet troops began to withdraw in stages beginning May 1988.

Mujahideen guerrillas at a machine gun nest fire at Soviet aircraft flying through the Jagdalak Valley in eastern Afghanistan.

Exit strategy

The Soviet exit was part of Gorbachev's overall strategy, intended to reduce the Soviet Union's crippling military commitments and improve relations with the West. Evacuating the Red Army was difficult, since it entailed transporting 80,000 men and large numbers of tanks and armored vehicles over dangerous terrain. Although the Soviet Union undertook some successful missions as face-saving exercises before withdrawing, they had no influence on the conflict. The mujahideen increasingly took the offensive. The communist regime managed to fight on without Soviet help until it was overthrown in 1992.

- **SEE ALSO**
  Pages 22–23: March 11, 1985
  Gorbachev Becomes Soviet Leader

- **FURTHER INFORMATION**
  Books:
  Afghanistan by Nikki Van Der Gaag (Wayland, 2007)
  Websites:
  news.bbc.co.uk/1/hi/world/south_asia/ 1569826.stm
  Concise profile of the recent history of Afghanistan

The Louvre "Pyramid" Opens

The Louvre in Paris is one of France's most famous buildings. Originally a royal palace, it houses a huge national art collection, including many great paintings such as Leonardo da Vinci's "Mona Lisa." In 1981, the French president, François Mitterand, commissioned American architect I. M. Pei to design a new structure to stand in the vast courtyard of the Louvre. Pei's creation, Le Pyramide, was officially opened on March 29, 1989.

The Pyramid actually consists of one large and two much smaller pyramids, made of sparkling, reflective glass covering a grid-like steel frame. The main structure stands 67 feet (21 meters) high and measures 108 feet (33 meters) along the base of each side. It serves a practical purpose, providing a new and spacious entrance to the Louvre, leading down to a large, light-filled lobby. Initially, many people criticized the Pyramid, feeling that its shape, materials, and transparency jarred with the stately, classical style of the Louvre. However, over time, Pei's Pyramid has become a famous and familiar part of the cityscape.

The Louvre Pyramid stands as a striking symbol of modernity in the courtyard of the Louvre museum.

Parisian projects

The Pyramid was one of many new buildings erected during Mitterand's presidency (1981–1995) as part of a single, ambitious program, Les Grands Projets (The Great Projects). They ranged from a monumental Great Arch containing offices to a modernistic park scattered with bright red buildings. A disused railway station was imaginatively transformed into a major art museum, the Musée d'Orsay (1986). And the Arab World Institute (1987), designed by Jean Nouvel, had an extraordinary south front filled with aluminium and glass panels. Thousands of "diaphragms" opened and closed in them, appearing and disappearing. They controlled the amount of light allowed into the building while also creating a fascinating visual spectacle.

La Grande Arche in west Paris was designed by Danish architect Johann Otto von Spreckelsen.

1980s buildings

By the 1980s, there was no single dominant style in architecture. New buildings often mixed styles, and advances in engineering enabled architects to produce highly unusual designs. The AT&T Building in New York (1984), designed by veteran American architect Philip Johnson, was a conventional skyscraper built in pink granite and decorated with pseudo-classical features. In contrast, the British architect Richard Rogers gave the Lloyds Building (1986), in the City of London, fantasy-like tall metal towers constructed around a central space, with pipes, lifts, and other utility features exposed on the outside. Such glamorous commercial projects were undertaken in many of the world's major cities and fit the dynamic atmosphere of the 1980s.

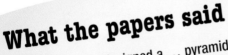

What the papers said

Ieoh Ming Pei ... designed a ... pyramid which, surmounting a grand underground entrance hall, has become a bigger spectacle than the Mona Lisa, and Paris's most controversial piece of modern architecture.... Though early reactions to the pyramid ranged from the amazed to the hostile, Mr. Pei remained confident that Parisians would learn to love his structure ... when they could see how useful a role it played in creating big, bright spaces below, and how reordering the museum around a new point of entry gave its rambling galleries a more logical and accessible shape.

Robert Cottrell, *Independent*, March 30, 1989

• **FURTHER INFORMATION**

📖 Books:
   The Louvre (Building World Landmarks) by Sudipta Bardan-Quallen (Blackbirch Press, 2005)

🖱 Websites:
   www.louvre.fr/llv/musee/
   alaune.jsp?bmLocale=en
   Louvre site with virtual tour of the Pyramid

Massacre in Tiananmen Square

Demonstrations in China's capital, Beijing, ended on June 4, 1989 when army units moved in and fired on the protesters, many of them students. The demonstrations were focused in and around the historic center, Tiananmen Square. The protests, attended by up to 100,000 people, had faced China's ruling Communist Party with a difficult decision. The leadership was split, since elements within the party and the army had some sympathy with the demonstrators. But the hardliners took control and used troops to crack down on dissent.

A new atmosphere

China had been ruled by the Communist Party since 1949. The communists, led by Mao Zedong, had established a powerful one-party state. Mao's 27-year rule was marked by often disastrous experiments that damaged China's society, economy, and foreign relations. His successor, Deng Xiaoping, set the country on a different course. People were encouraged to go into business for themselves, and foreign firms began to operate in China. The new atmosphere encouraged people's hopes for greater political freedom. They were further encouraged by Mikhail Gorbachev's reforms in the Soviet Union. Gorbachev's visit to China in April 1989 sparked the demonstrations in Tiananmen Square.

During the demonstrations, students carved a statue of the "Goddess of Democracy," a woman holding aloft a torch, which strongly resembled the famous Statue of Liberty in New York Harbor. Despite the hint of U.S. influence, the protesters may not have wanted to see China transformed

The assembled demonstrators hail the statue of the "Goddess of Democracy" in Tiananmen Square.

into a Western-style democracy. Nevertheless, they certainly hoped for greater openness and opportunities to express their opinions.

Just an incident?

The details of what actually occurred on June 4, are still unclear. The West immediately described it as "the Tiananmen Square massacre." To the Chinese authorities, it was "the June 4 Incident." Estimates of the number of dead vary wildly. The Chinese claimed that no student protesters were killed, only troublemakers who had tried to take advantage of the disorder. However, Western foreign correspondents in Beijing claimed that at least 2,000 civilians were killed. Whatever the truth is, the Chinese government's actions that day demonstrated that, unlike East European communist governments in 1989, it had no intention of giving way to popular protest. Despite tremendous economic growth and ever-increasing contacts with the outside world, China would continue into the 21st century as a tightly controlled single-party state.

A lone protester, known to the world as "Tank Man," heroically blocks the path of a tank convoy along the Avenue of Eternal Peace near Tiananmen Square.

eye witness

At four o'clock sharp, just before daybreak, the lights in the Square suddenly went out ... the front of the Square was packed with troops ... they lined up ... machine-guns in front of the Monument to the Heroes of the People.... The troops and policemen ... stormed the monument.... Some troops were kneeling down and firing. We had to retreat back up onto the Monument. When we reached it the machine-guns stopped. But the troops on the Monument beat us back down again. As soon as we'd been beaten down, the machine-guns started up again ... we escaped in the direction of Beijing railway station.

An anonymous Beijing student, New Statesman and Society, June 16, 1989

- **SEE ALSO**
  Pages 16–17: September 16, 1982 Massacres in Lebanon
  Pages 38–39: November 10, 1989 The Berlin Wall Comes Down

- **FURTHER INFORMATION**
  - Books:
    The Rise of Modern China by Tony Allan (Heinemann, 2003)
  - Websites:
    video.google.com/videoplay?docid= 1761062858590826090
    Dramatic video footage of the protesters clashing with the Chinese army

The Berlin Wall Comes Down

On November 10, 1989, for the first time in 28 years, East Germans crossed freely into West Berlin. Since 1961, West Berlin had been fenced off by a 11.5-feet-high (3.5-metre-high) concrete wall policed by armed guards ready to shoot anyone who tried to climb over it. The object of the wall was to prevent citizens of communist East Germany from fleeing to West Berlin, a small non-communist area deep inside East German territory. However, by 1989, the political situation was changing. On November 9, the East German authorities announced that the previously guarded checkpoints would be opened. Huge numbers of jubilant East Germans crossed the border. Many of them demolished sections of the hated wall and took away chunks as souvenirs. The event came to be called the fall of the Berlin Wall. Though it did not literally disappear, it had ceased to keep people apart.

East Germans eagerly clamber over the Berlin Wall after learning that they could cross freely into West Berlin for the first time.

Europe divided

Germany was divided in 1945, when each of the victorious Allies of World War II took control of one zone. Eventually, the U.S., British, and French zones were united as West Germany (the Federal Republic). The Soviet-held eastern zone became a communist state, East Germany (the German Democratic Republic). The pre-war German capital, Berlin, deep in the eastern zone, was similarly divided into West Berlin (part of the Federal Republic)

eye witness

There was activity all along the Wall, and the constant sound of hammering. People were beating the Wall with picks and chisels. The candles they brought shed a golden light.... When the men ... stopped hitting the Wall on our side, you could still hear sounds ... people were trying to break through from the Eastern side ... a tiny hole appeared, and then grew bigger. At last, we saw a hand come through the little gap.... A man on our side grabbed it and shook it. In all my life I had never thought anything like this might ... be possible.

John Simpson, *Twenty Tales from the War Zone* (Pan, 2007)

November 1989: Huge crowds of demonstrators gather in Prague, capital of the former Czechoslovakia, to demand change and to protest against the unpopular communist regime.

and East Berlin.

By this time, the Cold War had begun and a long frontier, nicknamed the "Iron Curtain," separated Western and Eastern Europe. Though stranded behind the Iron Curtain, West Berlin survived, and its existence caused the communist regime serious problems.

The curtain lifts

As in other Eastern European states, East Germany's communist government had been imposed by the Soviet army at the end of World War II. It was never popular, and huge numbers of East Germans fled by crossing into West Berlin. Finally, in 1961, the Berlin Wall was built to prevent further mass migrations. The wall served its purpose until Mikhail Gorbachev withdrew Soviet protection from East Germany and the other communist regimes in the late 1980s. In 1989, mass popular protests led to changes of government in Poland and Hungary. As the pressure built up, East Germany accepted the inevitable, and the wall came down. The tide of revolution swept on. By the end of 1989, East European communism had collapsed.

- **SEE ALSO**
  Pages 6–7: August 30, 1980
  Solidarity Is Legalized in Poland
  Pages 22–23: March 11, 1985
  Gorbachev Becomes Soviet Leader
  Pages 36–37: June 4, 1989
  Massacre in Tiananmen Square

- **FURTHER INFORMATION**
  📖 Books:
  The Fall of the Berlin Wall by Nigel Kelly (Heinemann, 2000)
  Websites:
  www.germany.info/relaunch/info/publications/infocus/9_November/wall_stories37.html
  Personal recollections of the fall of the Berlin Wall

MTV Debuts

At exactly 12:01 A.M. on August 1, 1981, a new television network was launched with the words, "Ladies and gentlemen, rock and roll." The network was MTV: Music Television. Its goal was to play music videos – short films accompanying a song or other piece of music – on television 24 hours a day, introduced by live hosts called VJs (for video jockeys). Within a few years, MTV had changed the music industry and made music videos a central part of popular culture.

Did Video Kill the Radio Star?

Music videos had been around since the 1940s, when jukeboxes played short video clips of musicians. During the 1960s, various performers, such as Ricky Nelson and the Animals, produced videos, and the Beatles' first film, *A Hard Day's Night* (1964), included scenes of them performing their songs. Many videos produced during the 1960s and 1970s were used to persuade people to buy records, but radio was the music industry's primary outlet. During the 1970s, though, the industry was in a slump with record sales and income from concerts declining. The time was ripe for something new and different – MTV.

The first video shown on MTV was, appropriately, "Video Killed the Radio Star" by the British group the Buggles. The song is about a singer, popular during the days of radio, whose career is cut short by television. However, MTV and music videos actually helped the industry by attracting viewers who tuned in to watch videos. This new attention to popular music translated into increased record sales. MTV provided a constant flow of videos, showing the more popular ones more often (similar to the way Top 40 radio works). A large number of 1980s rock bands were made popular by MTV, including Prince, Duran Duran, Bon Jovi, and The Police.

eye witness

The main ingredients in MTV's programming are "video records" or "videos": current recordings illustrated by 3- or 4-minute videotapes . . . in which rockers strut or act out their stuff. These are punctuated every few songs by the patter of veejays (video jocks). MTV also features some live concerts . . . and flashes of rock gossip . . . . The simulated performance clips tend to be dull and repetitive . . . . But the best videos enhance the mood of a song and expand TV's generally unadventurous visual vocabulary.

"Cable's Rock Round the Clock," *Time*, November 29, 1982

The original MTV VJs (video jockeys) were (left to right) Mark Goodman, Nina Blackwood, J.J. Jackson, Martha Quinn, and Alan Hunter.

The Network Changes

When MTV began, only a few thousand people in the New York area who had a specific cable TV system could watch the network. In 1982, MTV became available in Manhattan and Los Angeles, thus attracting more attention from the national media. The network was criticized in its early years for not featuring diverse kinds of music, especially black artists. In 1983, the network began to give heavy play to videos from Michael Jackson's album *Thriller*. MTV's association with Jackson helped popularize both the network and the performer. The network also began to feature different kinds of music, including rap, heavy metal, and alternative rock.

MTV is now seen in hundreds of millions of homes, on 150 channels, worldwide. Music, however, is no longer the network's main business. While MTV still plays some music videos, it now mostly broadcasts reality shows like *The Real World*. The network also airs programs on social, political, and environmental issues of interest to young people.

- **SEE ALSO**
  Pages 24–25: July 13, 1985
  The Live Aid Concerts

- **FURTHER INFORMATION**
- Books:
  MTV: The Making of a Revolution by Tom McGrath (Running Press, 1996)
- Websites:
  www.mtv.com
  MTV, for news on the music and entertainment industry, music videos, and the network itself

The Iran-Contra Affair Is Revealed

In the mid-1980s, the administration of President Ronald Reagan was rocked by the Iran-contra affair – two secret operations, involving actions that were either illegal or went against U.S. policies, to aid groups in two other nations. In November 1986, the public learned about the two parts of the affair: selling arms to Iran and then sending the profits to the anti-Communist contra rebels in Nicaragua.

The affair becomes public

On November 3, 1986, a Lebanese magazine reported that Americans had delivered a shipment of arms to Iran. At the time, Iran was holding seven Americans hostage. The Reagan administration's policy was not to deal with Iran. At first, the administration denied the story. However, in a televised address on November 13, Reagan admitted that arms had been sold to Iran to establish better relations with moderates there.

The second part of the affair, involving the contras, was made public on November 25. Reagan announced that he was firing a staff member of the National Security Council, Lieutenant Colonel Oliver North, for taking certain unauthorized actions, and that his national security adviser, Admiral John Poindexter, had resigned. Attorney General Edwin Meese revealed that some of the profits from the arms sales to Iran had been sent to the contras in Nicaragua – rebels who were trying to overthrow that country's government. Reagan believed that Nicaragua's Communist government was a threat. He favored the contras, but Congress had passed a measure that banned helping them, making the sending of funds illegal. Oliver North claimed that

On March 4, 1987, President Reagan gave a nationally televised address. He admitted that members of his administration had traded arms for hostages with Iran and funneled the profits to the Contras.

Poindexter knew he was sending the funds to the contras. North assumed that Reagan approved of the move – which the president denied.

Investigations

Reagan appointed a commission to investigate the matter. The commission concluded in 1987 that there was no evidence that the president sent funds to the contras, but he should have had better control over his staff and known what they were doing. Another investigation by independent prosecutor Lawrence Walsh concluded in 1994 that while there was no evidence that Reagan had broken the law, the president might have participated in or known about a cover-up. In 1989, North was convicted of obstruction of Congress and destroying government documents; his conviction was later overturned. In 1990, Poindexter was convicted on several counts including conspiracy and lying to Congress; his conviction was also overturned.

Lieutenant Colonel Oliver North gives evidence at the Iran-Contra hearings in Washington, D.C., during July 1987.

What the Chief of Staff said

[Attorney General Edwin Meese] came in. He said Mr. President, I got some bad news for you. . . . He said there's been a probable diversion of funds from the arms sales to Iran then diverted to the contras in Nicaragua. The president said I'll have to clean this up a little bit. Aw shoot, or words to that effect. The president actually turned white. He blanched and he said what could have been going through their minds. Why would they do this?

White House Chief of Staff Donald Regan, recalling the events of November 24, 1986, when President Reagan was told of the contra connection

- **SEE ALSO**
  Pages 10–11: November 4, 1980
  Reagan Is Elected U.S. President

- **FURTHER INFORMATION**
  📖 Books:
  The Iran-Contra Affair by Lisa Klobuchar (Compass Point Books, 2008)
  🖱 Websites:
  www.pbs.org/wgbh/amex/reagan/index.html
  The website of a documentary about Reagan

The *Exxon Valdez* Oil Spill

On the night of March 23, 1989, the oil tanker *Exxon Valdez* left the port city of Valdez, Alaska, bound for Long Beach, California. The tanker belonged to Exxon Corporation. Because of ice in the area, the tanker was traveling outside normal shipping lanes. Captain Joseph Hazelwood went to his quarters after handing control to two crew members and telling them to turn back into the shipping lanes. This was not done, and at 12:04 A.M. on March 24, the ship ran aground on Bligh Reef. Oil began to spill out of the ship. It would turn out to be the worst oil spill in U.S. history and one of the worst environmental disasters in the world.

The scale of the disaster

Hazelwood had violated Exxon policy by leaving the ship's controls, and the men left in charge were not certified to pilot a ship in that area. Over the next two days, some 11 million gallons (42 million liters) of oil spilled into the water, eventually reaching areas 460 miles (740 kilometers) southwest of Bligh Reef. Oil dirtied 1,300 miles (2,092 km) of shoreline in the once beautiful Prince William Sound. The Alyeska Pipeline Service Company and Exxon led the clean-up efforts. Storms in the area and high tides made clean-up efforts difficult and carried the oil over a larger area.

Two weeks after the disaster, the stricken oil tanker Exxon Valdez *is towed off Bligh Reef in Prince William Sound for repairs.*

An estimated 250,000 seabirds, 2,800 sea otters, 300 harbor seals, 22 killer whales, and billions of salmon and herring eggs died as a result of the spill. Volunteers and professionals worked to clean birds and sea otters that had become covered with oil.

Aftermath

In 1991, the federal government and the state of Alaska reached agreements with Exxon and Alyeska on damages caused by the spill. In all, Exxon paid $3.4 billion in cleanup costs, compensation claims, fines, and other expenses. In 1994, thousands of local fishermen and native people were awarded $5 billion in damages. This was reduced to $2.5 billion by an appeals court in 2006. In 2008, the U.S. Supreme Court reduced it further to $500 million.

Clean-up efforts went on for four years. Yet, by early 2007, more than 26,000 gallons (98,400 l) of oil still remained in the shoreline soil. In late 2007, researchers reported that two species, Pacific herring and pigeon guillemots, showed no signs of recovering to their levels before the spill. Other species, though, had recovered or were recovering. Commercial fishing, recreation and tourism in the area had not yet fully recovered.

Rescue workers hold an oil-covered cormorant that was caught in the Exxon Valdez *oil spill.*

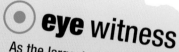

eye witness

As the largest oil spill in the history of the United States entered its second day, only a feeble containment effort had been mounted and a crowd of state, federal and oil company officials remained undecided about how to clean up the mess. A 32-square-mile, multi-hued sheen continued to float and spread atop the waters of Prince William Sound. . . . Unless the spilled oil can be dealt with, it is a near certainty that it will wash ashore somewhere in the Sound . . . .

Anchorage Daily News, March 25, 1989

- **SEE ALSO**
  Pages 28–29: April 26, 1986
  Accident at Chernobyl

- **FURTHER INFORMATION**
  Books:
  The Exxon Valdez *Oil Spill* by Elspeth Leacock (Facts on File, 2005)
  Websites:
  www.adn.com/evos
  Hard Aground: Disaster in Prince William Sound, a collection of material from the *Anchorage Daily News*

People of the Decade

Yasser Arafat
(1929–2004)
A Palestinian leader who, in 1969, became chairman of the Palestine Liberation Organization (PLO), bringing together most of the militant Palestinian groups hostile to Israel. Despite PLO terrorism, Arafat addressed the United Nations and skillfully publicized the Palestinian cause. After years of changing fortunes, in 1993, Arafat made a peace agreement with Israeli leaders that allowed for limited Palestinian self-rule in the occupied territories. In 1994, he became president of the Palestinian National Authority, but violent new conflicts troubled his later years.

Benazir Bhutto
(1953–2007)
The first woman to lead a modern Muslim state, Benazir Bhutto became prime minister of Pakistan in 1988–1990 and 1993–1996. As head of the Pakistan People's Party, she was opposed by conservative elements in Pakistan and by the army, which often intervened in politics. Both of her terms in office were controversially cut short. In exile from 1996, she returned to Pakistan in October 2007 but was assassinated two months later.

Deng Xiaoping
(1904–1997)
A veteran communist, Deng Xiaoping held high government office in China from the 1950s. Favoring moderate, realistic policies, Deng was in disgrace during the Cultural Revolution, launched in 1966 by China's leader, Mao Zedong. Deng gradually rebuilt his position, and after Mao's death (1976) he became Chinese leader and introduced new policies allowing more economic freedom. China prospered, but power remained with the Communist Party, which crushed the 1989 protest movement in Tiananmen Square.

Diana, Princess of Wales
(1961–1997)
In 1981, Lady Diana Spencer married the heir to the British throne, Charles, Prince of Wales, in a televised ceremony watched by a global audience of 750 million. The royal marriage quickly ran into difficulties, and Charles and Diana were finally divorced in 1996. However, Diana remained a popular figure, often in the news and admired for her charitable work. Her death in a car accident in 1997 sparked an astonishing display of public mourning.

Madonna
(1958–)
A musician and actress, Madonna became a pop sensation in the 1980s. She released her debut album in 1983 and went on to produce three number-one albums before 1990. She had a strong influence on young people's outlook and fashions, and the lyrics of songs such as "Material Girl" reflected the decade's emphasis on affluence and possessions. Often referred to as the "Queen of Pop," Madonna maintained her superstar status into the 21st century.

Ferdinand Marcos
(1917–1989)
In 1965, Marcos was elected president of the Philippines in Southeast Asia. Increasingly corrupt and dictatorial, he enriched himself while millions of Filipinos lived in poverty; the huge, gaudy shoe collection of his wife Imelda became particularly notorious. In 1986, Marcos was forced to hold an election following the assassination of a political rival, Benigno Aquino. Marcos claimed to have won, but popular anger forced him into exile, and the murdered man's widow, Corazon Aquino, became president.

François Mitterrand
(1916–1996)
Mitterand was president of France for a record 14 years (1981–1995), winning elections in 1981 and 1988 as the candidate of the Socialist Party. He strongly supported closer ties with Germany and other European powers and was a key player in the formation of the European Union in 1993. He also launched an ambitious building program that transformed large areas of the capital, Paris.

Martina Navratilova
(1956–)
The tennis star Navratilova left her home country of Czechoslovakia in 1975 and settled in the United States. She won the singles at Wimbledon in 1978 and dominated women's tennis for over a decade. During her career, she captured 167 championship titles, more than any other player, male or female, in history. She retired in 1994, making a brief return to doubles competitions in 2000. At a time when public figures revealed little about their sexuality, she became an outspoken campaigner for gay rights.

Oprah Winfrey
(1954–)
Coming from a poor background, Winfrey became one of the world's most influential women and the richest African American. Her talk show, *The Oprah Winfrey Show*, has been running since 1984. It has maintained a huge audience thanks to the introduction of new ideas such as Oprah's Book Club. Winfrey has taken up important issues, such as drug abuse, and has raised money for many causes, including help for New Orleans following Hurricane Katrina.

Glossary

autonomy Self-government that falls short of independence. Scotland and Wales, for example, run many of their own affairs but are finally answerable to the British parliament in Westminster (London).

bloc A group of states that are allies and generally act together.

Cold War The long period of hostility (roughly 1945–1990) between the United States and the Soviet Union and their respective allies. It is described as "cold" because there was no actual fighting between the two main powers, but a tense battle for influence and military superiority.

colony A territory ruled by a distant and usually more powerful state. India and Nigera were British colonies, and so were the 13 American colonies that revolted and formed the United States.

communism A political and economic system in which wealth and production are controlled by the state, supposedly for the benefit of all citizens.

conscript A citizen who must undertake compulsory military service.

containment boom Equipment that is placed in water and used to absorb and contain liquid by forming a gate around it.

contras Members of the counterrevolutionary force, backed by the United States, that tried to overthrow the government of Nicaragua during the 1980s.

decrepit Worn out through age.

depression A long-lasting economic crisis involving declining production, bank failures, and mass unemployment.

dictatorship A form of government in which a single person or small group has absolute power.

epidemic An outbreak of a disease that spreads quickly and more widely than would normally be expected. The World Health Organization declared AIDS an epidemic in the 1980s.

guerrillas Fighters who avoid open warfare, instead launching surprise attacks and then withdrawing quickly. Guerrilla tactics are particularly effective in difficult terrain such as mountains or jungles.

livestock Domestic animals that are kept for food or similar purposes.

martial law Military law, often imposed on an entire population during a real or pretended emergency.

militancy This describes the vigorous, sometimes violent, pursuit of political or other aims.

militia Citizens who are organized to fight but are not full-time soldiers.

mujahideen A term for Muslim fighters engaged in holy war (jihad), especially those who opposed the Soviet-backed regime in Afghanistan between 1980 and 1988.

NASA The National Aeronautics and Space Administration, the organization responsible for the U.S. space program.

PLO The Palestine Liberation Organization. It consists of a number of groups formerly dedicated to destroying Israel and now aiming to establish a Palestinian state.

radioactive This describes material that sends out radiation. Radiation is energy in the form of subatomic particles that are harmful to living things.

Red Army The army of the Soviet Union.

Republican A member or supporter of the Republican Party, one of the two main political parties in the United States. The other is the Democratic Party.

Roentgen A measure of radiation (see radioactive).

Royal Marines A unit of Britain's Royal Navy with specialist commando training.

sanctions Limits on trade with a particular country, usually imposed by the international community on regimes that behave unacceptably.

shares Any of the equal parts into which ownership of a company is divided.

skimmer A machine that separates a liquid or particles floating on top of another liquid, for purposes such as removing oil floating on water.

skirmish A small-scale fight, involving fewer men than a battle. Skirmishes often happen as a result of accidental clashes in which no clear military objective is involved.

Soviet Union Also called the USSR (Union of Soviet Socialist Republics), the Soviet Union was founded in 1922 as a communist state encompassing Russia and other nearby countries. It collapsed in 1991.

stagnant Not moving. The word is used in economics to describe lack of progress.

stalemate A situation in which neither of two opposing sides can gain the advantage.

strike A form of action undertaken by employees who refuse to work until their pay or working conditions are improved.

trade union An organization that represents some or all of the workers in a particular industry.

unilateral One-sided; a decision reached without the agreement of another concerned party.

Index  Page numbers in **bold** refer to illustrations